CONTENTS

Some words are shown in bold, **like this**. You can find out what they mean by looking in the glossary.

The Kingdom of Benin existed in an area of West Africa. It lasted from about AD 900 until 1897. Benin was one of the most powerful kingdoms in the region.

Today, there is an African country called the Republic of Benin. It was named after the old kingdom, but is not in the same place. The Kingdom of Benin was based around Benin City, and its **citizens** were a people called the Edo. Benin City is now part of a large country called Nigeria. The Edo still live in the same territory there.

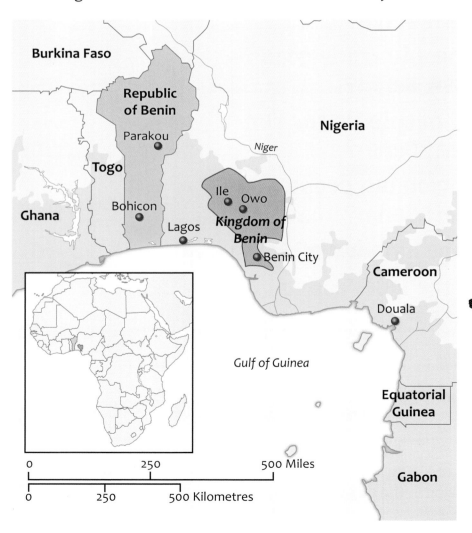

The Kingdom of Benin was not the largest in the region (that was the Mali Empire), but it was powerful and long-lived.

Daily Life in ANCIENT BENIN

Paul Mason

raintree
a Capstone company — publishers for children

Raintree is an imprint of Capstone Global Library Limited, a company incorporated in England and Wales having its registered office at 7 Pilgrim Street, London, EC4V 6LB – Registered company number: 6695582

www.raintreepublishers.co.uk
myorders@raintreepublishers.co.uk

Edited by Linda Staniford and Holly Beaumont
Designed by Philippa Jenkins
Original illustrations © Capstone Global Library Limited 2015
Illustrated by Oxford Designers and Illustrators; caption characters and pages 42-43 by Philippa Jenkins
Picture research by Gina Kammer
Production by Victoria Fitzgerald
Originated by Capstone Global Library Ltd
Printed and bound in China by Leo Paper Products

ISBN 978 1 406 29849 9 (hardback)
19 18 17 16 15
10 9 8 7 6 5 4 3 2 1

ISBN 978 1 406 29855 0 (paperback)
19 18 17 16 15
10 9 8 7 6 5 4 3 2 1

British Library Cataloguing in Publication Data
A full catalogue record for this book is available from the British Library.

Acknowledgements
We would like to thank the following for permission to reproduce photographs: Bridgeman Images: © Look and Learn/Private Collection/An English expedition eager to secure the precious spices are brought before the Oba, or King, McBride, Angus (1931-2007), 6, British Museum, London, UK/Benin Plaque, Nigeria (brass), Benin, 19, Pitt Rivers Museum, Oxford, UK/Interior of King's compound burnt during fire in the siege of Benin City, 1897 (silver gelatin print), Granville, Reginald K. (fl.1897), 41; Bridgeman Images/Werner Forman Archive: A plaque depicting a servant collecting fruit, one of many which decorated the palace of the Oba of Benin, cover, An arm ornament in the form of a leopard, part of a ceremonial outfit of the Oba of Benin, 23 An ivory hip pendant depicting an Oba (Benin king) and two attendants, 22; Corbis, 10, © Stapleton Collection, 7; Getty Images: Eco Images, 20, Eco Images, 24, Print Collector, 37, The Washington Post, 17, UniversalImagesGroup, 26, Werner Forman, 13; Glow Images: Heritage Images/Werner Forman Archive, 9, Werner Forman Archive, 8, Werner Forman Archive/British Museum, London, 32; iStockphoto: mrundbaken, 27; Newscom: Africa Media Online/Andrew Esiebo, 15, Andre Held/akg-images, 34, Arco Images G/picture alliance/Diez, O., (top) 21, DanitaDelimont.com Danita Delimont Photography/Ancient Art & Architecture, 36, EPA/STR, 38, Eye Ubiquitous, 31, Pierre Alozie/Design Pics, 14, REUTERS/AKINTUNDE AKINLEYE, 33, Robert Harding/Jenny Pate, 12, Werner Forman/akg-images, 5; Science Source: Jerry Mason, 35; Shutterstock: Bildagentur Zoonar GmbH, (top) 18, Four Oaks, 16, Harley Couper, (bottom) 18, Sura Nualpradid, (bottom) 21; SuperStock: imageBROKER, 28

Cover image: A bronze plaque showing a servant collecting fruit. One of the Benin Bronzes, it would have once have decorated the Edo's palace in Benin City.

Every effort has been made to contact copyright holders of material reproduced in this book. Any omissions will be rectified in subsequent printings if notice is given to the publisher.

The Ogiso and the founding of Benin

The Kingdom of Benin began under the rule of a line of mysterious kings called Ogisos. *Ogiso* means "King of the Sky" in the Edo language. Traditional stories showed the Ogisos as godlike beings who helped to create Edo society.

The Ogisos ruled from about 40 BC–AD 1100. The exact dates are not known because there are no written records of this time.

The rise of the Oba kings

After the Ogiso rulers came the Oba. Each of the first Obas was chosen by a group of important chiefs, called the Uzama. Once he had been picked, though, the Oba had complete power. He was the head of Edo society, and the army, land and trade all fell under his control.

This brass head shows an Oba wearing rows of coral beads around his neck and a coral bead headdress.

EWEKA 1

Eweka I was the first Oba. He came to power in about 1180. Eweka is said to have been the son of an Ogiso, who had been **banished** to a neighbouring territory, Yorubaland. When he was asked to return to Benin as ruler, Eweka called himself Oba, a Yoruba word for "king".

Warrior kings

From the 1400s, Benin began to grow, expanding its territory under the rule of a line of Obas who are sometimes called the "Warrior Kings".

The armies of the Warrior Kings had two big advantages over their rivals. The first was that Benin had become a wealthy kingdom, so its soldiers were the best equipped in the region. The second was that the Kingdom began trading with European countries.

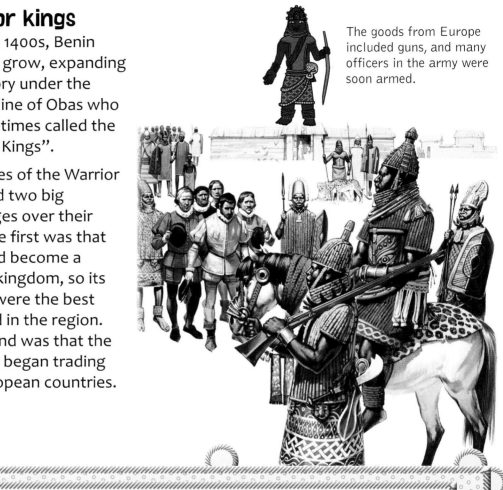

The goods from Europe included guns, and many officers in the army were soon armed.

OBA EWUARE

Sometimes also called "Ewuare the Great", he became Oba in about 1440. Once in power, Ewuare fought wars against neighbouring territories, starting the expansion of Benin's territory.

Life for ordinary people

Life for ordinary people changed very little from the early days of the Ogisos until the Kingdom fell in 1897. The people lived in houses that looked the same, played music and games, grew food, made goods to sell and traded at the markets. They also held many of the same beliefs.

In fact, many of the activities people carried out in ancient Benin still go on in Edo villages today.

HOW DO WE KNOW?

The people of Benin traditionally recorded events in stories (see page 16 for more on storytelling). These were passed down through the generations by being told, rather than written down. Written records only began when Europeans started visiting the Kingdom, in the late 1400s, and recording what they saw. Our understanding of what Benin was like before that time comes from archaeological evidence, stories and our knowledge of modern Edo life.

The Kingdom of Benin area was thick with forest. Most people lived in villages in the forest. In fact, Benin is sometimes called the "Forest Kingdom". The forest played an important role in villagers' lives.

The tropical forest that covered much of Benin was especially dangerous at night, when leopards prowled silently beneath the trees.

Villages in the forest

Within the village, each family had its own home with a small space outside. They also had a plot of land that they farmed. There was a village shrine, and a place where the villagers gathered in the evenings to listen to the storytellers.

The Edo people lived in villages partly for protection. Together they could defend themselves from attack by other Edo, or even raiders from elsewhere. Living in villages also kept the people safe from wild creatures and the evil spirits it was said lived in the forest.

Although the forest was dangerous, it was also useful. You could grow crops there, and gather food, firewood and building materials. It was also where plants for treating illnesses grew.

RULING THE LAND

Villagers didn't own their land — Benin's ruler owned it on behalf of the whole kingdom. This gave the Ogiso or Oba tremendous power.

Even the leopard had to accept the power of the Oba, as shown in this plaque.

Growth of the cities

As time went on, the Kingdom's most important and powerful villages grew. They began to take control of other nearby villages. Eventually, they became cities. The greatest of them all was Benin City.

This is a European artist's impression of Benin City, from 1668.

Benin City

Benin City was a thriving place. European visitors described a city with wide, straight roads. There were many palaces and large houses, built around square courtyards – a similar style to the ones used in ancient Rome.

The city was where the Kingdom's ruler and his helpers and advisers lived. They held meetings with foreign **diplomats**, made trade agreements, passed laws and managed the day-to-day life in the Kingdom. The royal palace was so large that European visitors sometimes struggled to find their way around.

Benin City was also home to lots of other people. These included many of Benin's trade **guilds**, artists and craftspeople.

The Benin Walls

Surrounding Benin City were moats and huge earth walls, which defended the city against attack. Reports do not agree on the size of the Benin Walls, but they may have been up to 20 metres (66 feet) high in some places. Some estimates say the walls were 16,000 kilometres (9,950 miles) long, contained more material than the Great Pyramid of ancient Egypt and took 150 million hours to build.

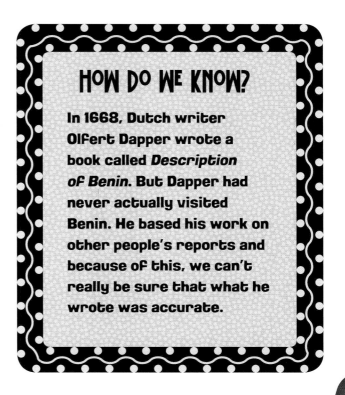

HOW DO WE KNOW?

In 1668, Dutch writer Olfert Dapper wrote a book called *Description of Benin*. But Dapper had never actually visited Benin. He based his work on other people's reports and because of this, we can't really be sure that what he wrote was accurate.

Divisions in society

For ordinary people in ancient Benin, there were two key divisions in society:

1. **The division between men and women.** From quite a young age (about seven years old), males and females did different jobs.

2. **The division between younger and older.** People in the Kingdom had great respect for age. For example, the village chief was usually the oldest man, since his wisdom was thought greater than that of anyone younger.

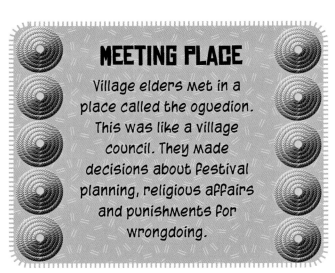

MEETING PLACE

Village elders met in a place called the oguedion. This was like a village council. They made decisions about festival planning, religious affairs and punishments for wrongdoing.

The Kingdom's market sellers were mainly women – just like in Edo lands today.

The male and female worlds

Men went through three ranks as they grew older. First came ikpolo ughe, for boys who were not yet adults. Their main responsibility was to look after the village, for example by sweeping up and mending the paths.

In Benin City, older people are still respected for their great experience.

Next came the eghele, grown men who were still young. These men were the main workforce, doing jobs such as defending the village from attack and preparing it for festivals.

Last were the edion and odionwere. Both groups were older men, but the odionwere were more important and led meetings of the village elders. They represented the ruler's authority.

Among women there were three ranks. Younger girls were expected to run errands and to do other jobs for older women. The unmarried women were the main workers and did most of the household chores. Finally, older, married women were in charge of the household, making sure it ran smoothly.

Imagine not having to go to school! Well, in ancient Benin children didn't. But that doesn't mean they ran around playing all day. Instead children were taught by their families, and through stories.

Family Lessons

The people usually lived in large family groups. Children learned skills from other members of their family. This included parents, brothers and sisters, plus uncles, aunts, cousins and more-distant relatives.

Most villagers did some farming, so nearly everyone learned about planting and harvesting crops. But if a boy's father or uncle was a blacksmith, potter or musician, for example, he might also learn one of those skills. If there was a guild for his new skill, he might one day join that, too.

People in ancient Benin had to work hard to clear the forest for farming. Today, most people in modern-day Nigeria still work on the land.

Girls learned from their mothers, older sisters and aunts. Women ran the household, so girls learned to clean, prepare food and cook. Younger girls fetched firewood and water. They also took goods to market, some even becoming wealthy traders. They decorated pottery, and learnt to weave and sew. Benin was famous for its stripy coloured cloth – it was extremely popular with Europeans. In turn, the Edo wanted red and metallic fabrics, especially velvet and silk, from the Europeans.

HOW DO WE KNOW?

Our knowledge of weaving in the Kingdom of Benin is based partly on Edo weavers in the 21st century. Some still make cloth using traditional looms, and the cloth they make matches descriptions of the goods European traders bought in Benin. We can guess from this that some patterns have been made in a similar way for hundreds of years.

Storytelling

Imagine life without a TV, video games or tablets. What on earth would you do with your time? In ancient Benin, children were kept busy a lot of the time with chores and learning new skills. They were also allowed time to play games, of course. But in the evenings, the villagers could gather to hear the Edo equivalent to TV and radio: a storyteller.

ANIMAL TALES

Many of the kingdom's most popular stories included animals. Stories about the ant kingdom or the undersea world were particular favourites. In other stories, great chiefs were associated with powerful animals. For example, one chief, who tried (and failed) to defeat the Oba in the 1500s, was said to be able to turn himself into an elephant.

Lessons from stories

The stories were fun, or sometimes scary – and they often also contained a lesson. This kind of story is called a **fable**. For example, a story might tell of a farmer who was late coming back from his fields. He gets caught in the forest after dark, is chased by an angry ghost and is never seen again. The lesson is clear – don't go into the forest at night or you might not come back.

Children still enjoy a good storytelling session today.

THE STORY OF TOUCAN

This story was told by Edo people to show how the world was made.

First, the land was covered in water, with just a tree sticking up. In the tree lived Toucan.

The two sons of Osonobua, father of the gods, were canoeing across the water. Toucan asked the first son to make him a snail shell. He did this, and out poured a stream of sand, which built up to make the land. To test the land's firmness, the sons sent Chameleon to walk on it — and even today, Chameleon still walks with a hesitating step.

Osonobua made his youngest son the ruler of Benin, which was at the centre of the land. Osonobua himself went to live in the spirit world, which exists where the sky and Earth meet.

The sons of fearsome Benin soldiers would probably follow them into the army.

XVIII, 4.

98
I - 15
39

Palace apprenticeship

The Kingdom of Benin had one further way of educating its boys (especially boys from important families): a system called a palace apprenticeship.

Some jobs at the palace were **hereditary**. For example, when a palace chief (a government official who lived in the royal palaces) died, one of his sons might become a palace chief in his place.

Some palace apprenticeships went to boys who didn't have royal officials as relatives. These boys were chosen either as a reward for one of their relatives, or because they were unusually good at something. For example, a young man who knew several languages might be brought to the palace to train as a translator.

For men, there were a variety of jobs in the Kingdom, anything from professional wrestling to the priesthood. Opportunities for women were more limited. Women were expected to marry, then look after the home and children.

Most ordinary people worked as farmers to grow food. This would either be eaten or taken to market to sell.

Typical ingredients in Edo cooking – the same today as hundreds of years ago.

Farming the land

For meat, people kept cattle, sheep, goats and chickens. They also fished and gathered shellfish. The main crops were yams, cassava, plantains and cocoyams. Alongside these were rice, beans, okra, gourds, peppers, and fruit from the forest.

Some crops were valuable for trade. One of these was peppercorns, which were used to make pepper. People also grew cotton, which was used to make the region's famous cloths.

Big business

Ordinary villagers could trade their goods within the Kingdom, but the Oba and his officials controlled trade with Europeans. This is one of the reasons why the Kingdom's rulers became so rich. For example, the Oba was able to buy pepper at local prices. He would then sell it to Europeans at higher prices.

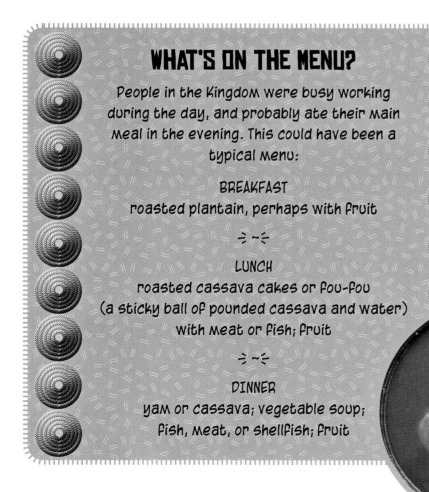

WHAT'S ON THE MENU?

People in the Kingdom were busy working during the day, and probably ate their main meal in the evening. This could have been a typical menu:

BREAKFAST
roasted plantain, perhaps with fruit

≥ ~≤

LUNCH
roasted cassava cakes or fou-fou
(a sticky ball of pounded cassava and water)
with meat or fish; fruit

≥ ~≤

DINNER
yam or cassava; vegetable soup;
fish, meat, or shellfish; fruit

Other jobs

Farming wasn't the only job available in the Kingdom. Some people combined farming with other work, such as building. Others earned a living by selling their skills or products.

Benin needed all kinds of workers: artists, musicians, traders, weavers, builders, soldiers, priests, blacksmiths, fishermen, government workers and storytellers, for example.

Carved objects like this, showing the Oba and his two helpers, were highly valued in the Kingdom of Benin.

JOBS FOR WOMEN

Women couldn't do every type of job in the Kingdom, but they were not restricted to their homes. For example, women were market traders, and made pottery for use at home. They also wove the cloth for which Benin was famous. This cloth was traded throughout Africa, long before Europeans ever visited.

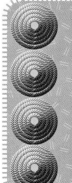

OGISO ERE

Ogiso Ere is said to have ruled from about AD 16-66. Some say Ere invented the guild system, at first for wood and ivory carvers. Ere may also have introduced some of the **symbols** of African kings, the stools, crowns, swords and badges of power other rulers later used.

The trade guilds

Many of the most skilled workers in the Kingdom lived in Benin City. They were members of guilds, organizations of people who all did the same job. The guilds ensured that workers were properly trained. Membership of guilds often passed from father to son.

Each guild lived in a particular area of the city. If you wanted a new sword, for example, you went to the area where the Guild of Blacksmiths was based. For carved ivory, you needed the Guild of Carvers. And if you were feeling sick, you'd need to head for the Guild of Doctors. There were guilds for lots of different jobs. They included leather workers, drummers, dancers and even leopard hunters.

As the king of the forest, the leopard often appears in carvings made for the Oba.

Bronze-making

One of the most important jobs in the Kingdom was making "bronzes" for the Oba. These were figures and plaques that were actually made of brass. The royal palaces were decorated with hundreds, maybe thousands, of these bronzes.

Trade with Europe was important for the bronze-makers. Until European traders arrived, there had been a shortage of raw material for making bronzes. European traders brought with them bracelets called manillas, which were made of bronze or copper. These could be melted down and used for making bronzes.

These men from modern-day Benin City are making bronze in a traditional way.

OGISO UWA

Ogiso Uwa is said to have ruled from about AD 767-821. Some stories say that bronze-making developed in Benin during his reign. Uwa's daughter Emwinkururre was apparently the first to wear brass rings on her wrists and ankles.

The Benin Bronzes

The Benin Bronzes are a group of metal plaques that originally hung in Benin City. In 1897, they were **looted** by British forces (find out more about this attack on page 41). The Bronzes were taken back to Europe, where they were sold to museums around the world.

The Bronzes show a variety of subjects. Some feature life at the royal court. Others show events from Benin's history, such as great military victories. Many feature the Oba.

HOW DO WE KNOW?

The bronze figures and plaques that survive from ancient Benin are an important source of information about what life was like there. However, the bronzes do not show scenes from ordinary village life. They are mostly concerned with the rich and powerful, and generally show life at the royal court or images of the Oba.

There were two important types of trade in ancient Benin. First was trade within Benin, at the Kingdom's markets. Second was trade with other countries, which was controlled by the Oba and his officials.

Market trading

It was usually women who took goods to market, and some became skilled (and sometimes wealthy) traders as a result. Edo markets still run in a similar way today. They are an occasion for meeting friends, as well as for trade, and people like to dress up in fine clothes.

An official, usually a man, is in charge of the market. His jobs include telling people where they can set up their stall. The earlier you arrive, the better the space you get. Some families send along a representative at dawn to try to get a top spot.

If a time traveller from the Kingdom visited a modern Edo village, lots of the festivals, stories and activities would seem familiar.

Markets in ancient Benin would have had a variety of goods on display, including animals and left-over crops. Some stalls may have sold pottery, cloth and other household goods. Whatever you were buying, you could expect to have to negotiate the price.

Did you know?

Traditionally, people in Benin used cowrie shells as money. These were **imported** from the far-away Indian Ocean or East African coast, and as such were considered valuable. People sometimes threaded 40 or 100 shells onto strings, making something similar to a £10 or £20 note.

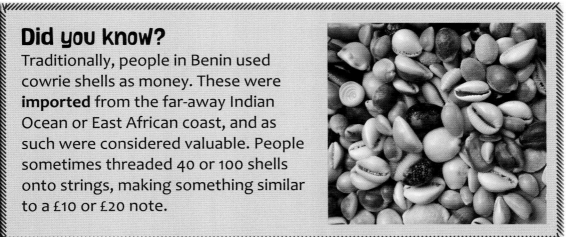

OGISO OHUEDE

Ogiso Ohuede is said to have ruled from about AD 871-917. During his rule, the Kingdom suffered from terrible **inflation** when a huge stash of cowrie shells was discovered. Having so many extra cowrie shells around made them worth less, and the number of cowries it took to buy anything shot up.

Cowrie shells were once used as money in many parts of Africa.

Foreign trade

Benin had many trade links with African and European territories. The Kingdom sat where trade routes from all across Africa met. Goods such as ivory, cloth, carvings on ivory and wood, pepper and bronzes were in high demand.

For international trade, bronze manilla bracelets were used as money. These manillas were usually made in Europe, but were used as money throughout West Africa for hundreds of years. Eventually people used cowries only for small purchases, and manillas for larger ones. Manillas only stopped being legal money in 1949.

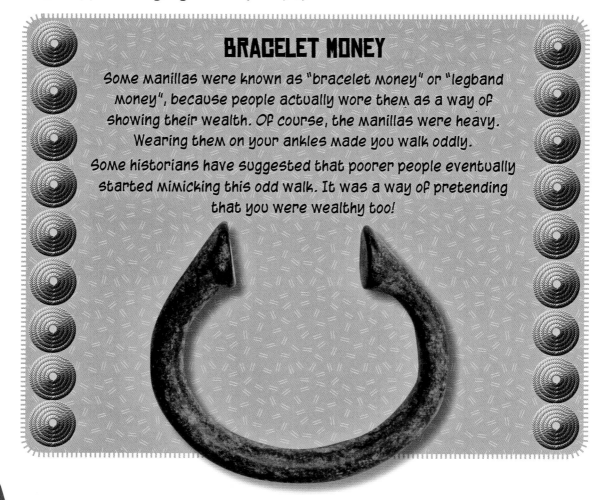

BRACELET MONEY

Some manillas were known as "bracelet money" or "legband money", because people actually wore them as a way of showing their wealth. Of course, the manillas were heavy. Wearing them on your ankles made you walk oddly.

Some historians have suggested that poorer people eventually started mimicking this odd walk. It was a way of pretending that you were wealthy too!

The trade in people

One of the things European traders most wanted to buy was people. Once bought, these people would be loaded on to cramped ships and taken to the Americas. Those who survived the voyage would almost certainly spend the rest of their lives living in **slavery**.

The trade in people is a **controversial** subject. Historians disagree about exactly what happened in the Kingdom of Benin. It is clear, though, that the Oba and his officials were involved in the trade. Money from the slave trade helped the Oba equip his soldiers with guns. This made the army better able to capture territory and prisoners – some of whom were sold to the slavers.

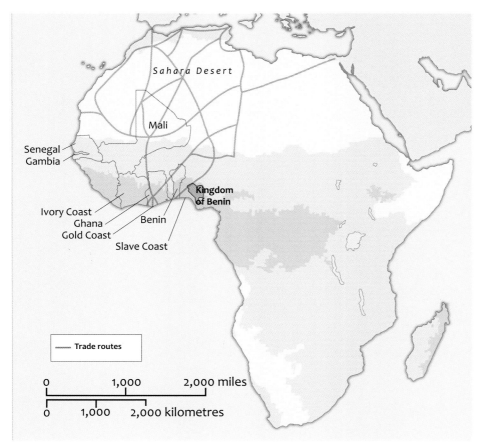

The Kingdom of Benin was at the meeting place of several important trade routes.

Until they were about seven, children in the Kingdom had lots of time for games. And although adults in Benin worked hard, even they had spare time for enjoying themselves.

Children's games

We can guess that children in Benin played similar games to kids everywhere, games such as catch. One you might not know is a chase game played by many Edo children. This is how it works:

The players stand in a circle, all looking inward. One person is outside the circle, holding an object (it doesn't matter what it is). He or she creeps around, trying to put the object down behind someone in the circle without them noticing. The aim is to run around the outside of the circle at full speed and get back to the object without being caught by the person it was behind. That way, you get their space, and they are outside the circle.

HOW DO WE KNOW?

There are few exact records of the games people played. We have to piece together information from a variety of sources. Some activities are shown on bronzes or in statues. Others are mentioned in stories. Many of the same games and sports are still played by Edo people in Nigeria today.

MANCALA

Mancala is a popular game throughout West Africa, and was played by people in ancient Benin. Mancala is also known by other names. It seems simple, but is tricky to play well.

For two players, the game needs a wooden board with two carved rows of six scoops. If you don't have a board, you can make these scoops in the ground. Each scoop contains four pebbles.

The first player picks up the contents of a scoop. Going anti-clockwise, he or she then drops one pebble in each scoop until the pebbles run out. The players take turns doing this.

If your last pebble lands in a scoop with three in it already, you get to collect all four pebbles and bank them. But if any of your *other* pebbles lands in a scoop already containing three, your opponent banks those.

Once there are only four pebbles left or fewer, the winner – the person with the most pebbles in the bank – is decided.

Music

Music was a big part of the Kingdom's life, especially festivals. There were lots of different **percussion** instruments, such as drums, bells and clappers. One kind of clapper was called an ukuse. It was bit like a maraca, and was used to get the gods' attention.

Musicians would often accompany important people and the army.

OGISO ODION

Odion, the 16th Ogiso, ruled from about AD 567-584. He was famous as a lover of songs and music, and is said to have been a storyteller before becoming Ogiso.

Sports

Although farming was tiring, people in the Kingdom still enjoyed active sports. Some of these traditional sports are still played in Nigeria today.

A game called langa has always been popular with young people. In this, you hold one leg up behind you with your hand. Your opponent does the same. Then you try to topple one another: the winner is the one who stays upright.

Among adult men, wrestling matches were a popular contest of strength and skill. People may also have taken part in a form of boxing similar to one from northern Nigeria, called dambe. In this, boxers fight with their punching hand wrapped in cloth and a knotted rope. Their other hand is used as a shield, or for grabbing the opponent. Kicking is allowed, and sometimes the fighters even wrap their leading leg in a metal chain.

Traditional wrestling is still popular today.

Religion was an important part of life for people in ancient Benin. Their homes had shrines in honour of the family's ancestors. They also believed in a range of gods.

The real world and the spirit world

Edo people thought there were two parallel worlds, the real world and the spirit world. These were not completely separate: one could reach into the other. Spirits could affect the human world, causing both good and bad events. For example, the ghost of an ancestor who felt neglected might spoil someone's crops, or make a child sick.

Priests and the spirit world

The Edo people believed that priests could communicate with the gods and spirits. They could find out why something had gone wrong, for example a family's crops failing. They could also give people advice on how to put things right, such as by giving an ancestor some extra honour or attention.

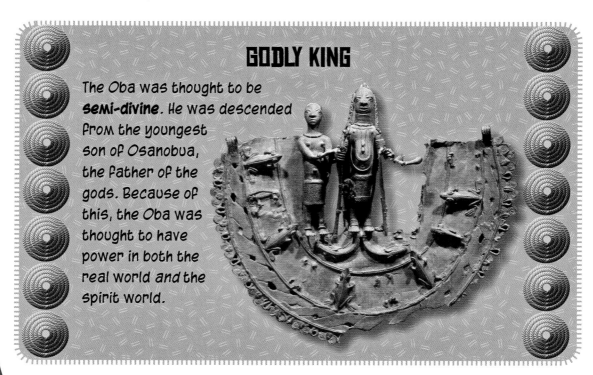

GODLY KING

The Oba was thought to be **semi-divine**. He was descended from the youngest son of Osanobua, the father of the gods. Because of this, the Oba was thought to have power in both the real world and the spirit world.

Truth trials

Sometimes even a priest couldn't say for sure what had caused a misfortune, or who was responsible for a crime. If there was a **suspect**, the priest might hold a truth trial.

The suspect might be told to take an oath of innocence, which included terrible penalties from the spirit world if he or she was lying. Another possibility, for really serious offences, was being given poison to drink. Since the poison was often fatal, anyone who lived must have survived because they were innocent.

The poisonous Calabar bean was fed to people in an attempt to determine their innocence or guilt.

Gods of ancient Benin

People in Benin recognized many gods. Not all gods were worshipped in every part of the Kingdom, but everyone knew the most important ones. First among the gods was Osanobua, father of the other gods.

Osanobua lives in a great spirit-world palace, and doesn't concern himself with the world of humans. He leaves that to the other gods, his offspring. These include:

NAME: Olokun

COLOUR: White

RESPONSIBILITIES: Olokun is Osanobua's eldest son and is god of the oceans. He is also the bringer of children, and the source of wealth and good luck. Olokun is associated with beauty and exceptionally beautiful women often became his priestesses.

NAME: Ogiuwu

COLOUR: Black

RESPONSIBILITIES: Ogiuwu is god of the underworld and bringer of death via his messenger Ofoe. Ofoe is represented as having no body, only arms and legs: he needs only legs to chase his victims, and arms to hold on to them. Then he drags them back to the underworld for Ogiuwu.

NAME: Ogun

COLOUR: Red

RESPONSIBILITIES: Ogun is the god of iron, and is associated with people who use metal tools. Soldiers, craftspeople, farmers and hunters all pay special attention to Ogun. The two **ceremonial** swords worn by the Oba are symbols of his connection with Ogun.

NAME: Osun

COLOUR: Red

RESPONSIBILITIES: Osun is a forest god, whose products can be used to treat illnesses and who is linked with healing.

HOW DO WE KNOW?

Many of the bronzes featuring the Oba demonstrate his connections with the world of the gods. For example, crocodiles and pythons were linked to the water god Olokun, and are often shown with the Oba. The Oba is also sometimes shown with **mudfish** legs, showing how he, like the mudfish, can survive in two different worlds at once.

In this image, the Oba is shown with mudfish legs. These symbolize his power over the different worlds.

Festivals in ancient Benin

Every day, people honoured gods important to them. A blacksmith, for example, might pray to Ogun each morning. The Kingdom also held big festivals in honour of the important gods. Work stopped and people dressed in their best clothes. The Oba led the ceremonies. He dressed in his royal finery, and his symbols of power were on show for all to see.

These women are making music in praise of the Oba, as part of the modern-day Igue festival.

Harvest festival

Most people in the Kingdom grew their own food, so the harvest festival was especially important. The festival was held at the time of the new yam harvest, and lasted seven days. The chief gods honoured were Ogun and Osun. They were associated with farming and things that grew in the rainforest.

The king's festival

Even more important than the Harvest festival was the nine-day king's festival, called the Igue festival. It is still celebrated by Edo people today, between Christmas and New Year. During the festival, the Oba's powers and links with the gods were renewed, and he blessed the people. Foreigners were not allowed to set eyes on the Oba during the Igue festival.

HOW DO WE KNOW?

We know about the symbols the Oba carried to show his power because many of them survive. These include:

- Two types of sword, called the eben and the ada. The eben had a broad, leaf-shaped blade, while the ada had a curved end.

- Beautifully carved ivory objects. The whiteness of the ivory represented purity, and its long-lasting nature represented the Oba's long reign.

- Coral beads, a symbol of the Oba's authority and links with the gods. It was said that any prophesies or curses the Oba issued while holding coral beads would be sure to come true.

The Kingdom of Benin finally ended in 1897. The Kingdom had been weakened by **civil wars** and loss of trade. Benin also had valuable **resources**, such as rubber, palm oil and ivory, that the world's most powerful country, Britain, wanted.

Britain and the Kingdom

Britain mainly wanted Benin's supplies of rubber, which came from large numbers of rubber trees. There was a big demand for rubber to make tyres for motorcars, bikes and other vehicles.

In 1892, Britain tried to make Benin its protectorate, which would have given the British control. But the Oba hadn't asked to be protected by Britain! The disagreement continued until, in 1897, the Oba's forces killed a group of British officials.

POWERFUL EMPIRES

During the 1800s, European governments used their powerful armies to take over other parts of the world. In Africa, this race to take over other countries became known as "The Scramble for Africa". The newly conquered territories were called empires. The biggest empire of all belonged to Britain.

The Punitive Expedition

That year, Britain sent 1,200 soldiers to Benin, in what was known as the Punitive Expedition. In revenge for the killing of British officials, the soldiers burned down large parts of Benin City, and took away all the art and treasures they could find. They forced the Oba into **exile**. The British now controlled the country.

After the Kingdom

Benin became part of a larger British-controlled area, called Nigeria. In 1901, Nigeria officially became part of the British Empire. Then in 1960, Nigeria became an independent country. The heart of the old Kingdom of Benin became Nigeria's Edo State. The Oba has returned, and his palace is in Benin City.

The treasures of ancient Benin have ended up in private collections and museums all around the world.

A day at the Igue festival

My name is Adesuwa, and I am nine years old. Mostly I spend my time helping my mum and aunties – but today is a special day. Today it's the most important day of the Igue festival, in honour of the Oba.

During the festival, people spend a lot of time visiting each other. Our door is always open for visitors. We women were up **VERY** early this morning to help prepare food – before the sun came up! My father is an important man, and we were expecting many guests.

Of course, we didn't actually have to prepare the food ourselves – the household servants did that. Still, my mum always wants to know what's going on. If the soup isn't spicy enough, or the rice isn't cooked properly, someone gets it in the neck!

Once the food was organized, we started to get ready for the Oba's parade through the streets. He's been preparing for today for many weeks, and hasn't been seen. Mum had sent servants down to guard our places: we moved in and settled down, and it wasn't long before the Oba appeared.

He was dressed in fine clothes, with the swords and other badges of office on display, and a great sunshade held over his head. The people cheered so loudly it was deafening. We all cheered too, until the Oba disappeared around a corner. People chatted a while, and then we headed for home.

There was food – MOUNTAINS of food, great cauldrons of stew, roasted meat, fish, everything! There was music and dancing. One of the dancers was so good that my father gave him some money. I can still hear the noise now... but I HAVE to go to bed. I'm SO tired – and there will be more festival to enjoy tomorrow!

AROUND 40bc

The first Ogiso, Ogiso Igodo, begins his rule over the new Kingdom of Benin.

AD 16-66

Ogiso Ere rules the Kingdom of Benin. He develops the first guild system, for wood and ivory carvers.

767-821

Ogiso Uwa rules Benin. Bronze-making develops during his reign.

900S-1100S

The Ogiso rulers began to make Benin City a great centre for trade and government, and expand the Kingdom's territory by conquering other lands.

1180-1440

The rule of Obas begins. The Obas strengthen the Kingdom and establish many of its customs, but do not greatly expand its territory.

1440

Ewuare the Great becomes Oba. He strengthens the Kingdom's armies and fights wars to expand its territory. At this point Benin starts to become an empire.

1489

Portuguese traders seeking new trade routes across Africa arrive at the coast of Benin. This opens the way for other Europeans to visit.

1668

Dutch writer Olfert Dapper writes *Description of Benin*. He bases his work on the accounts of church missionaries and explorers.

1700S

From 1700 onwards, the Kingdom's power begins to decline as powerful chiefs fight to become Oba. Fighting civil wars weakens Benin's armies, and the Oba's control over the region decreases.

1800S

In the early 1800s, a succession of countries ban the slave trade, and slavery eventually becomes illegal. Benin's trade in rubber, palm oil and cloth brings an improvement in the Kingdom's wealth and influence.

1897

After several years of trying to persuade the Oba to make his country a British protectorate (which basically meant handing control to the British), the British send a military force called the Punitive Expedition to the Kingdom. They destroy Benin City, exile the Oba to Calabar and take control of the country. It later becomes part of Nigeria.

1901

Nigeria becomes part of the British Empire.

1949

Bronze manilla bracelets stop being legal money.

1960

Nigeria gains its independence.

GLOSSARY

banish force to go and live elsewhere

ceremonial used during ceremonies, for example religious or royal events

citizen person who lives in a particular country

civil war war between forces from the same country

controversial leading to disagreement or argument

diplomat official representing their country's government in other countries

empire group of countries that are all ruled by the government of one of the countries

exile being banned from living in your own country, usually as a punishment

fable story that has a message, and which often features animals as characters

guild organization of skilled workers who do a particular type of job, such as metalworking

hereditary passed down within a family, usually from parent to child. For example, the job of Britain's monarch is a hereditary one.

import buy something from another country

inflation increase in the cost of everyday items such as food and clothes

loot stolen from a place during or after violence has happened there, for example after an army has attacked and captured a town

mudfish fish that is able to leave the water and crawl about on land

percussion musical instrument that is played by hitting or shaking it

plaque flat plate, usually made of metal, wood or pottery, with an outer surface showing an event or person

resource supply of something useful, such as oil, gold or farmland

semi-divine somewhere between a human and a god, with characteristics from both

slave person who is not free and has to work for an owner for no payment

suspect person who it is thought might have committed a crime

symbol badge or sign of something. For example, a king's crown is a symbol of the fact that he is a king.

Books

Benin 900–1897 CE (The History Detective Investigates), Alice Harman (Wayland, 2014)

Diary of an Edo Princess; Ehi, Edo Warrior Chief; and Uki at Ukpe Festival, Fidelia Nimmons (CreateSpace, 2013)

Discovering the Kingdom of Benin (Exploring African Civilizations), Amie Jane Leavitt (Rosen Publishing, 2014)

Places to visit

British Museum
Great Russell Street
London
WC1B 3DG
www.britishmuseum.org

The British Museum is where many of the Benin Bronzes ended up. Many of the bronzes owned by the museum are on permanent display in the Africa Wing.

Horniman Museum
100 London Road
London
SE23 3PQ
www.horniman.ac.uk

The Horniman Museum hosts storytelling sessions featuring tales from Benin, and schools or large groups can book a study visit about the Kingdom.

Pitt-Rivers Museum
S Parks Rd
University of Oxford
Oxford
OX1 3PP
www.prm.ox.ac.uk

The Pitt Rivers Museum is in a beautiful old building, worth visiting on its own. The Museum owns masks, bronzes and ivory carvings from the Kingdom of Benin.

INDEX